John Cabot

Neil Champion

Heinemann Library
Chicago, Illinois

Designed by AMR
Illustrated by Art Construction and James Field
Originated by Ambassador Litho Ltd.
Printed in Hong Kong by Wing King Tong

05 04 03 02
10 9 8 7 6 5 4 3 2

Library of Congress Cataloging-in-Publication Data
Champion, Neil.
    John Cabot / Neil Champion.
        p. cm. -- (Groundbreakers)
    Includes bibliographical references (p.) and index.
    ISBN 1-58810-046-4 (lib. bdg.)   ISBN 1-58810-370-6 (pbk. bdg.)
    1. Cabot, John, d. 1498?--Juvenile literature. 2. America--Discovery and
exploration--English--Juvenile literature. 3. Explorers--America--Biography--Juvenile
literature. 4. Explorers--England--Biography--Juvenile literature. [1. Cabot, John, d.
1498? 2. Explorers. 3. America--Discovery and exploration--English.] I. Title. II. Series.

E129.C1 C48 2001
970.1'7--dc21
                                                            00-058140

Acknowledgments
The author and publishers are grateful to the following for permission to reproduce copyright
material: Bridgeman Art Library, pp. 5/Index, 7, 8/Roger-Viollet, 10, 13, 15, 18/Victoria & Albert
Museum, 19, 20, 21, 23, 26, 31/The Stapleton Collection, 33/Bristol City Art Gallery, 35/British
Library, 38/Bristol Museum, 40/National Portrait Gallery, Ireland; Corbis, pp. 14, 30, 41; Hutchison
Picture Library, p. 4; Mary Evans Picture Library, pp. 11, 12, 27, 28, 34, 39; Science Photo Library, p.
29/St. Mary's Hospital; The Art Archive, pp. 6, 22, 24, 25; The Slide File, p. 36; Tony Stone Images, pp.
9, 17.

Cover photograph reproduced with permission of Mary Evans Picture Library.

Every effort has been made to contact copyright holders of any material reproduced in this book.
Any omissions will be rectified in subsequent printings if notice is given to the publishers.

Some words are shown in bold, **like this.** You can find out what
they mean by looking in the glossary.

Contents

Who Was John Cabot?

You can see Genoa and Venice on the map on page 43.

John Cabot was a great explorer, though we know very little about his life. He was probably born in Genoa, a port in what is Italy today, around 1450. He died 48 years later on a voyage from England towards Greenland. His Italian name was Giovanni Caboto (*caboto* means "seaman"), but when he moved to England, he changed it to Cabot. He became a citizen of Venice in 1476, and was described by someone at the time as "a lower-class Venetian, of a fine mind, very expert at **navigation.**"

This is the port of Genoa as it looks today, on the Mediterranean coast of northwest Italy. John Cabot was born here about 550 years ago.

The problem of the past

John Cabot was one of the leading explorers at the start of an age of great European geographical discovery. In the 1490s, he made three sea voyages from England under the **patronage** of King Henry VII, looking for the **Northwest Passage.**

We know very little of John's childhood. His father was probably named Egidius Caboto, but we do not know what he did for a living. We do not know who his mother was. The few written records that have come down to us relate to his voyages. However, we can fill in some of the blank spaces of his life from our knowledge of the places where he lived and the lives of other people at the time.

Cabot and North America

John Cabot's great claim to fame is that he set foot on North American territory after a sea voyage from England of some 35 days. The year was 1497. He was sent by King Henry VII to find the elusive sea route to China and India through the Northwest Passage.

Instead, just like the better-known Christopher Columbus a few years before him, Cabot bumped into a huge area of land. He had no idea that an entire continent existed between his home in Europe and the **Orient.** He thought, like most of the people at the time, that if you sailed west, you would eventually come to China and India.

The Vikings may have reached American shores 500 years before John Cabot. They sailed in open boats, so the crew could not have escaped the weather.

Going even further back, the Irish monk Brendan may have landed in America in the 6th century. A poem written 1,000 years ago describes his voyages to fabulous islands. No doubt they would have been extraordinary journeys. Brendan set sail in a coracle, a small vessel made from animal skins, designed for shallow waters around the coast of Ireland.

YOU CAN FOLLOW JOHN CABOT'S JOURNEY ON THE MAP ON PAGES 42–43.

Records from the 15th century come in the form of royal decrees, documents issued by the pope (as shown here), church records, letters, and ships' logs, which recorded the details of the voyages.

John Cabot's World

From about 1461, John Cabot lived in the great **city state** of Venice in what is now Italy. He would have seen from an early age the tremendous benefits of trade with the fabulous East. Venice had a **monopoly** on most of this trade and became the richest city in Europe. However, the **Age of Exploration** was getting under way in Europe. One of the main motives behind these voyages was to find new routes to the East. Countries such as Spain and Portugal wanted their share of Eastern riches.

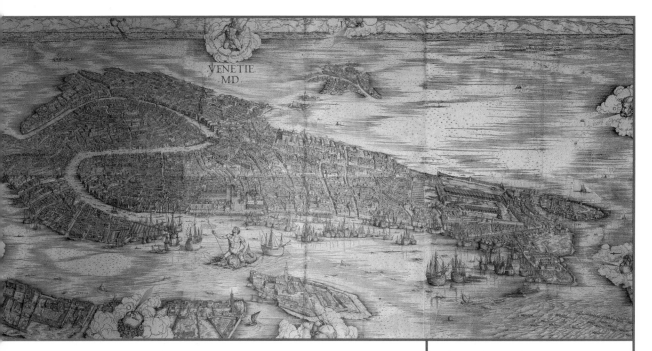

The Renaissance

Cabot lived over 500 years ago in a world that was moving from the **Middle Ages** into the **Renaissance.** This was an exciting and energetic time to be alive.

This is an engraving of Venice. In the 15th century, Venice was the most prosperous city in Europe, earning its wealth from trade with the East.

Discoveries in fields such as science and medicine, art and architecture were taking place at a rapidly growing pace. The science of **navigation** improved, as did the skill of ship design. These enabled people to venture further from home by sea than ever before. Cabot grew up in this exciting world and quickly learned the skills of a **navigator** and sailor. Unknown lands awaited those daring to take on the long and dangerous sea voyages. Cabot was one who dared.

New trade routes to the East

For hundreds of years, Europeans had obtained their spices, silk, precious stones, and perfumes from the East by way of the **Spice Route and Silk Road.** The **merchants** who traveled them crossed many countries, having to cope with such dangers as deserts, high mountains, and attacks by robbers. In 1453, when Cabot was three years old, a great battle took place that was to change things. The **Muslim** Turks, the great enemies of Christian Europe, captured the great Christian city of Constantinople (now Istanbul, in Turkey). It stood in a very important position on the silk and spice trading routes, and its capture blocked the way by land to the East for European merchants. Rulers in Europe began to finance voyages by sea to discover other ways to trade with the East, bypassing the old land routes.

One of the most famous merchants was Marco Polo, who traveled with his father and uncle from Venice along the Silk Road and Spice Route to China nearly 200 years before Cabot was born. He stayed in China for seventeen years, working for the emperor. When he finally returned to Italy, he wrote a book about his adventures and all the wonders he had seen.

This 16th-century painting is of the siege of Constantinople (present-day Istanbul) by Muslim Turk soldiers under their ruler, Mehemmed II. The city came under their power in May 1453.

Early Life

You can see where Genoa, Venice, Constantinople, and Cyprus are on the map on page 43.

For most of the **Middle Ages,** Genoa was a powerful **republic.** It traded with Eastern Mediterranean countries in the profitable silk and spice markets. However, after the Turks captured Constantinople in 1453, Genoese **merchants** turned to trading with North African countries. John Cabot was three years old when all this upheaval began in his home city. Genoa's power declined shortly after it lost its trade with the East. Maybe the young Cabot took this lesson to heart. For most of his adult life he was engaged in finding sea routes to the East, recognizing just how important its riches were for people in Europe. There is a saying in Latin: "A Genoese, therefore a trader."

This is a 15th-century painting of the trade in exotic goods from the East, of which John Cabot would have seen a great deal, in both his hometown of Genoa and the city of Venice, where he lived as a boy and young man.

Moving to Venice

Venice was also a republic. It was the great trading rival of Genoa. The Cabot family moved here around 1461, when John was about eleven years old. Unlike Genoa, Venice managed to survive the capture of Constantinople. The Venetians made peace with the Turks, which allowed them to keep a small part of Constantinople, from where they could carry on their business.

Venice controlled trade with the East, making it the richest city in Europe for a time. Venetian merchants built fantastic houses on the canals of the city. They held magnificent parties and feasts. For the young Cabot, the city must have been one of the most exciting places to be brought up in at that time.

8

Education

John Cabot could both read and write. He would have been taught at a Catholic Church school. He was probably fluent in his native Italian dialect as well as in Latin, the language of the church, law, and government. He must have learned English at some stage, though not at school. English was not an important language in the 15th century, outside England. He would have picked it up from English sailors or in England itself. Cabot also lived in Spain for some time, and therefore we can assume he learned the Spanish language as well.

These are the remains of a Venetian fortress on the island of Cyprus in the Eastern Mediterranean, where they had an important base.

THE WEALTH OF THE EAST

Spices, which fetched high prices, came from the Spice Islands (now called the Moluccas, or Maluku). They included nutmeg, cinnamon, ginger, and black pepper. People used spices to improve the flavor of food, which was difficult to keep fresh. **Ambergris** and musk from animals that lived in the East were used to make perfume. Silk came from China. Gold and precious stones came from India and Sri Lanka. Beautiful eastern carpets and dyes for clothes also fetched high prices.

Learning His Trade

Venice, a thriving center of trade, launched Cabot on his career. Throughout his life he would remember and honor this **city state.** When later, in 1496, he set foot on the shores of what was probably Nova Scotia or Newfoundland, he raised the flag of St. George of England and the standard (emblem) of St. Mark of Venice. He had moved to Venice with his family when he was about eleven. He grew up among **mariners** and **merchants,** people who worked in the very trades that would occupy his life. We know that he came to be regarded by people who knew him as a highly skilled sailor, **navigator,** and **cartographer.**

This painting is of Venice in the late 15th century, when John Cabot lived there. At the time, it was the richest and most powerful city in Europe.

Life in Venice

John Cabot probably lived in Venice until the late 1480s—a period of over 25 years. He learned his trade and made his name in this city. There are various documents from this time that refer to him or his family. One mentions his father, Egidius, and a brother, Piero. Another says that John, or Giovanni as he was called there, borrowed from his wife, Mattea. He probably married Mattea in the early 1480s. Between 1482 and 1484, he was involved in at least ten property deals around Venice.

Other documents tell us that he had three sons, Ludovico, Sebastian, and Sancio. Sebastian was to become a great explorer in his own right.

Travel

Cabot traveled extensively for a merchant company in the Eastern Mediterranean, the Middle East, and even as far as the Black Sea. He would have met many Arab traders bringing precious goods out of the East. Cabot was no doubt fascinated by their tales of far-away countries that Europeans had heard of but very few had ever visited. His imagination must have been fired by this contact with the world that made Venice so rich. How much richer it (and he) would be if only he could trade directly with Indian and Chinese merchants! John Cabot, like many adventurous and resourceful men of his day, was motivated by a desire to make money.

*This early 20th-century engraving shows Arab (**Muslim**) traders and European (Christian) merchants in the 15th century doing business together in the markets of the Middle East.*

11

Training as a Mariner

YOU CAN SEE THE PORTS THE VENETIAN GALLEYS SAILED TO ON THE MAP ON PAGES 42–43.

In the 15th century, Venice was at the forefront of new ship design. **Galleys** had been used in the Mediterranean for hundreds of years. The Venetians, motivated by the enormous wealth they were making from trade, enlarged these ships to cope with the sheer volume of goods they were transporting. It is on board these new galleys that John Cabot would have set out on his trading journeys. About twenty such ships went to sea each year, sailing to ports such as Constantinople, Alexandria, Cadiz, Lisbon, Bruges, and Southampton. The **merchants** who owned or **chartered** them bought goods in one place and sold them at a profit in another. The ships were also used to take travelers to the Holy Land (Palestine, where Jesus Christ had lived and died), as they were strong enough to withstand the rougher seas of the Atlantic Ocean, at least during the summer.

VENETIAN GALLEYS

Venetian galleys had three masts and sails but could be rowed over short distances. They could carry about 220 to 275 tons of **merchandise** and used a crew of around 200 men, which was expensive. Later ships relied more on sails and less on manpower, so they were cheaper to run.

This Venetian galley is painted on a 15th-century tile.

Life on board a ship

Cabot and other crew members who
sailed the Mediterranean Sea would
have had a tough life. Conditions were
very cramped, especially for the

This 16th-century map of the
Mediterranean Sea shows the North
African coast, southern Spain, France,
and Italy.

ordinary deck hands. Men of more importance, such as Cabot
himself, acting on behalf of a merchant, would have had a little
more living space. The Mediterranean is an ideal sea on which to
learn the craft of sailing. Being almost entirely enclosed, it
seldom has big waves. The climate, certainly in the summer
months, is mostly calm and predictable. So sailing on this sea was
easy compared with sailing the Atlantic Ocean.

Fact and fiction

John Cabot lived in a world very different from our own. No
maps showed the entire world—much of it was unknown. Those
maps that existed were never totally accurate. **Cartographers**
worked slowly and could not keep up with all the new
discoveries being made. No one even knew for sure if the world
was round or flat, or if such things as dragons and sea monsters
existed just over the horizon. Books from the period talk of
many fabulous things of this kind, based not on truth or
observation, but conjured up by the imagination.

13

Cabot Moves to Spain

You can see where Valencia is on the map on page 43.

Around 1490, at the age of 40, John Cabot moved with his wife, Mattea, to Valencia on the Spanish Mediterranean coast.
A record from Valencia, dated 1492, states, "We have been informed by Johan Cabot the Venetian, that he arrived at the city two years ago, and during this time he has considered whether on the beach of this city a port could be constructed."

Granada, in southern Spain, was one of the last strongholds of the Muslims on mainland Europe. It was recaptured by Ferdinand and Isabella of Spain in 1492.

Cabot was by now an experienced seaman. One reason for his move to Spain was to be closer to the Atlantic Ocean, where a route to the East was being sought. The fact that he was also enquiring about building a port at Valencia shows that he was looking at several ways to further his career. He almost certainly continued life as a **merchant** and seaman.

1492

The year 1492 was a very important one, for Spain and for Europe as a whole. It saw the success of the military campaign by the Christian king and queen, Ferdinand and Isabella, to rid their kingdom of the **Muslim Moors.** The Muslim threat was overthrown in Spain, although, as we have seen, it was growing in the Eastern Mediterranean. The incentive to find a sea route going west to reach the riches of the East became even stronger.

Ferdinand and Isabella asked Christopher Columbus to carry out a voyage of exploration. He sailed west in 1492. But instead of India and China, he found the West Indies, though he did not know it. John Cabot was no doubt fired with ambition by Columbus's discoveries.

Did Cabot and Columbus meet?

The famous Columbus passed through Valencia, where Cabot was then living. Did they meet? Both men were born in Genoa, at about the same time. They were both master sailors and adventurers. They had both come to Spain through their ambition to sail west to find India and China. They had so many things in common, but, sadly, we will probably never know if they actually met. However, we do know that Cabot's plan to build a port in Valencia was turned down by the authorities.

This is a 15th-century painting of King Ferdinand and Queen Isabella, who united all of Spain against the Muslims and fought a successful campaign to expel them.

SPOILS FROM A NEW WORLD

When Columbus returned from what he thought was India, he was wise enough to bring back proof of his exotic travels. This included four natives ("Indians"), parrots, spices, unknown plants, and plenty of gold artifacts. These astounded the court of Ferdinand and Isabella and made all of Spain dream of fabulous riches.

15

Cabot and Exploration

Perhaps fired up by the fame and success of Christopher Columbus, Cabot decided that he should find funding for his own voyage across the mighty Atlantic Ocean. His first choice was to seek help near at hand and from the nations that were most interested in Atlantic voyages. He arranged an audience (meeting) with the king of Spain and the king of Portugal, to see if either would be interested in backing him. He certainly had an impressive record, having gained vast experience sailing in the Eastern Mediterranean, trading with peoples from all over Europe and Asia.

Major setback

However, his applications were turned down by both countries. Spain now had Columbus, who was planning more voyages of discovery. Portugal aimed to sail around Africa and then on to India. Portuguese sailors already had a lot of knowledge of the West African coast. They had set up trading colonies in the Cape Verde Islands, Guinea, and Ghana. They had reached the Congo by 1482, and in 1488, Bartolomeu Diaz had sailed around the Cape of Good Hope. In 1498, Vasco da Gama reached India by sailing around Africa, proving their ideas to be sound.

PORTUGAL

Mediterranean Sea

ASIA

CANARY ISLANDS

ARABIA

INDIA

CAPE VERDE ISLANDS

GUINEA

GHANA

AFRICA

CONGO

SRI LANKA

Indian Ocean

N

Atlantic Ocean

W

E

S

Cape of Good Hope

Key
- Diaz (1488)
- Da Gama (1498)

This map shows the routes taken around Africa by Bartolomeu Diaz and Vasco da Gama.

Cabot looks to England

Once again John Cabot would have had to face hard decisions. He had his wife and three sons to consider. The goals he had in mind when he moved himself and his family to Spain had not been achieved. He must have felt very frustrated. The world was opening up around him. All the new exploration was being done by two countries, Spain and Portugal, which had coastlines that jutted out into the wild Atlantic Ocean.

Cabot must have sensed that exploration was the key to the future. Ships were now being constructed that could withstand the battering of storms. The skill of **navigation** had developed enough to allow **mariners** to sail out of sight of land and still have some idea of their position and direction. These were enormous strides forward, comparable to modern people finding they had the technology and skills to travel to the moon. Cabot had all the skills. But he had no commission, and we must assume that he was not rich enough to finance a major voyage himself. What could he do? Which European monarch could he now approach with his plans? The answer was England and its king, Henry VII.

The Portuguese set off along these shores, on the Atlantic coast, in the 15th century, looking for ways to increase their trade and their territory.

Cabot and Henry VII

Henry VII (1457–1509) was the first Tudor king of England, being the son of the Welsh nobleman, Edmund Tudor. He came to the throne by defeating King Richard III at the Battle of Bosworth Field in 1485. England was not a particularly important country in Europe at this time. Its population was under 3 million. The capital city, London, had only 50,000 people living in it. Spain and France were far larger and more powerful. However, Henry VII had ambitions for his nation. Most people worked on the land. Harvests were good throughout the second half of the 1480s, so his reign started well. Most of the wealth of the country came from exporting wool and woolen cloth to other European lands.

English shipping

Ship-building in England was in decline in the 1480s. Edward IV (1442–83) had created a Royal Navy, but this was half its original size by the time Henry came to the throne. **Merchant** shipping was used in times of need, such as war. But even merchant vessels had dropped in number. By the time Cabot arrived in England, Henry VII had set about changing all this.

This wood carving of King Henry VII of England, who became John Cabot's patron, was probably made in the 15th century.

THE MERCHANT ADVENTURERS

The Merchant Adventurers was a company, or **guild,** set up in London in the early 15th century. By the time John Cabot had moved to England, it was a very important trading company, organizing the export of wool to the Netherlands. It became rich and influential in matters of trade and exploration.

The king had passed two laws, called the Navigation Acts, in 1485 and 1489. These were designed to encourage English ship-building and trade by allowing merchants who used English boats to pay a lower rate of tax. Henry had also built the first European dry dock in Portsmouth, on the south coast of England, where ships could be taken out of the water for repairs. He further helped the navy by supporting the iron and cannon- and gun-making industries.

This is a late 15th-century woodcut of London, which was a city of some 50,000 people at that time.

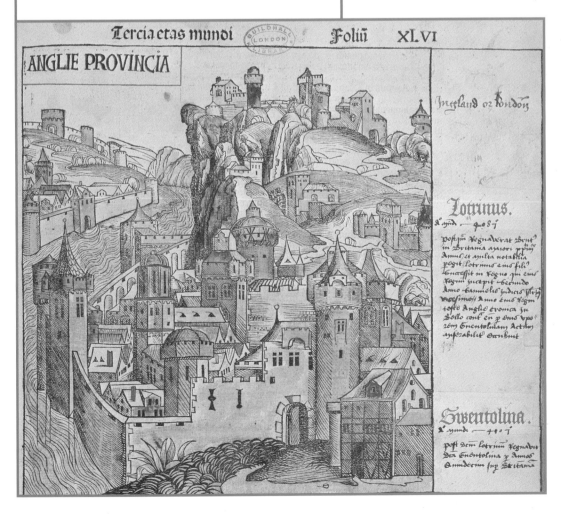

Cabot in the West Country

YOU CAN SEE WHERE BRISTOL IS ON THE MAP ON PAGE 43.

John Cabot settled in Bristol in the West of England either late in 1494 or very early the following year. Why did he choose Bristol as the place from which to relaunch his career as a master **mariner** and exploring **merchant?** At that time, Bristol was the second most important port in England, after London. It is situated on the Bristol Channel, which leads directly out into the Atlantic Ocean, and was therefore a perfect base from which to launch an exploration. The population was about 10,000, which is small by today's standards, but was significant then. Bristol merchants were very wealthy and powerful, and Cabot needed to gain their respect and interest if he was to get his project off the ground.

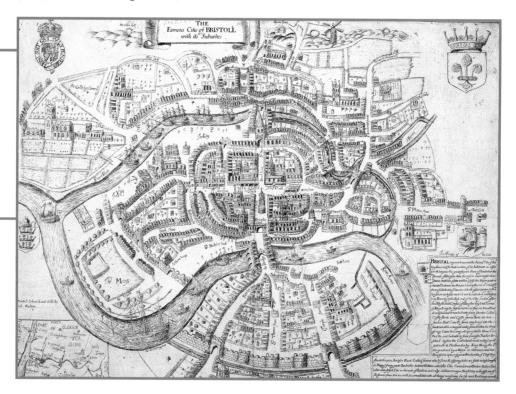

This map of the port of Bristol is from the 17th century. Cabot made his home here late in 1494.

THE WEALTH OF BRISTOL

Bristol earned its money from the sea. It did this in three main ways. Rich merchants owned ships that traded all over Europe, taking wool to sell and bringing back wine, spices, sugar, perfumes, carpets, tapestries, and precious stones. There was also a great deal of regional trade around the ports of England and Ireland. Fishing was the third important business, with Bristol boats going far into the Irish Sea and Atlantic Ocean to catch cod and other fish.

Bristol's reputation

The saying "ship-shape and Bristol fashion" comes from the fact that the ships of Bristol merchants were generally high-quality vessels, kept trim and in good order. It was in the owners' interests to do so. Ships were expensive and so were trading voyages. If a ship was lost at sea with all its cargo, the merchants involved would be ruined, not to mention the possible loss of life. The town's seamen were also held in high regard by the rest of the country. They were skilled in navigating the tricky waters of the Bristol Channel, which has one of the world's largest differences between high and low tide. They had good knowledge of the deep waters of the Atlantic. The port had a good reputation and it was important for trade, both local and international, that this situation continued.

This is a 19th-century painting of the Bristol Channel. It is a notoriously difficult place to navigate a ship, requiring great skill and care on the part of the ship's captain.

This was the town that Cabot chose to settle in. It would appear he made a good choice. It was nowhere near the size or importance of Venice or Genoa, or even Spanish Valencia, but it was growing, it was inhabited by people who knew the sea, and it was very close to the Atlantic Ocean.

Cabot Makes His Mark

Between 1488 and 1489, Bartolomew Columbus had gone to Henry VII of England on behalf of his brother, Christopher. He was hoping to get the king to finance a voyage out west. Henry turned down the request, and therefore lost out on one of the most important voyages of discovery. As we know, Christopher Columbus found favor at the court of Ferdinand and Isabella of Spain, and sailed to fame in 1492. When John Cabot moved to England with plans to upstage Columbus by finding a shorter, more direct route to the Indies, Henry perhaps felt that he should not pass up this second opportunity.

Christopher Columbus (1451–1506) was born in Genoa, where John Cabot was born about a year later.

In Cabot's words:

Cabot wrote to the king on March 5, 1496:

"To the king our sovereign lord: Please it your highness to your most noble and abundant grace to grant unto John Cabot, Citizen of Venice, Lewis, Sebastian and Sancio, his sons, your gracious letters patent under your great seal . . . And they shall during their lives pray to God for the prosperous continuance of your most noble and royal estate long to endure."

22

Cabot's contribution

It is thought that John Cabot brought very important charts and maps of the sea with him to England, which possibly no one in that country had seen before. He also brought with him his skills as a **navigator** and his knowledge of the best seafaring practice of the main **maritime** nations of Europe—Spain, Portugal, and Italy. He would have been able to tell of his adventures in the Eastern Mediterranean, meeting people from Asia and trading in exotic produce. There can be little doubt that he would have soon made his mark. The king would have been unable to resist the opportunities this Genoan-born **merchant** sailor presented.

RECORDS OF THE TIME

How do we know what little we do know about Cabot's life at this time? There are a few records made during his period in Bristol that have survived. One such is his rent book, which shows that he lived in St. Nicholas Street in Bristol. A letter to the king, and the king's **patent,** which gives Cabot and his sons permission to embark on voyages, also survive. We can guess from this that Cabot's sons were following in their father's footsteps, learning **navigation** and sailing skills. We know that Sebastian Cabot became an important sailor, **cartographer,** and explorer.

This 17th-century navigation chart was used by sailors to plot their course across the wide sea.

A Great Commission

King Henry VII of England issued his **patent** commissioning John Cabot to engage on a voyage into new territory in 1496. In it he makes clear that he does not want Cabot to offend Spain or Portugal by sailing south to lands that those nations were investigating. He says that lands occupied by "heathens and infidels" (by which he would mean any non-Christians) are fair game, but that any lands already inhabited by "Christians" (which would mean Spanish or Portuguese) were not. John Cabot had obtained what he had been hoping for all these years—a monarch's word of command to sail across the Atlantic Ocean, looking for new lands and a new sea route to the Indies. In London, he had presented his case to the king for a route to the East that was shorter than Columbus's route. A quick look at a globe will show why Cabot thought his route would be shorter. Having won his case, he could now look for ships and men in Bristol to accompany him on his first voyage into the unknown.

This is a 16th-century drawing of a Portuguese ocean-going ship. Fleets of these ships sailed to India, and Henry VII's letter of patent states clearly that Cabot was not to offend them in his own search for a route to the East.

Cabot's ships

The main ocean-going ship of this period was the three-masted **caravel.** It was very small, needing only about twenty men to crew it. One big problem for Cabot was the fact that the king did not back the venture with money from the royal **treasury.** Cabot would profit handsomely from any land and treasure obtained on the voyage, but he needed financing to get started. He probably went to the wealthy **merchants** of Bristol, whom he already

knew. However, he took only one ship on his first voyage, which may tell us that he was not very successful, at first, in obtaining the backing he needed. His two other voyages were better provisioned, with more ships.

This is a reconstruction of Christopher Columbus's caravel, the Santa Maria. *He sailed in this small craft in August 1492 on his epic voyage to the New World.*

Cabot Prepares for His Voyages

John Cabot made his first voyage in 1496, taking only one ship. This ended in failure, and he returned to Bristol having discovered nothing except perhaps that he would have to prepare better next time. A letter written by John Day explaining the reasons for failure (see box) shows that Cabot may have departed in haste, taking few supplies and not checking his crew properly. He could do nothing about the weather, but a more prepared expedition might have been able to ride the conditions out and continue on its mission. Some people think he left so quickly to get ahead of his rival Christopher Columbus.

A ship for success

Cabot spent the winter with his family in Bristol, probably preparing for his second attempt. This time he meant to get it right. He may well have commissioned a ship to be built especially for the voyage. This was the *Matthew*. It was built of English oak, taken from the Forest of Dean and the Wye Valley, on the Welsh borders. The timber was transported to Bristol by cart and boat for the **shipwrights** to start building the vessel, no doubt under Cabot's watchful, experienced eye. It took many men to work on such a project. The ship had three masts, and was built to the tried and tested **caravel** design.

King Ferdinand and Queen Isabella of Spain are saying farewell to Christopher Columbus at the dockside in 1492. Columbus's success on this voyage was no doubt a great inspiration to Cabot.

There is evidence that maps and charts were not used by English seamen until Cabot arrived. He introduced the type of map developed for **navigation** in the Mediterranean. However, Bristol fishermen did sail far into northern waters looking for the cod that formed an important part of people's diets at the time. There is plenty of evidence that these men used written notes that described how to make a journey from one place to another.

Fishermen from Europe may have even reached the shores of North America before Cabot, in 15th-century vessels such as these, but there is no record of such a voyage.

In John Day's words:

John Day was probably a spy living in Bristol, in the pay of the Spanish, though we know little about his life. Writing in late 1497 or early 1498, he gives some reasons for the failure of John Cabot's first voyage:

"Since your Lordship wants information relating to the first voyage, here is what happened: he [John Cabot] went with one ship, his crew confused him, he was short of supplies and ran into bad weather, and he decided to turn back."

Setting Sail

John Cabot's ship, the Matthew, *was built especially for him in Bristol for his second voyage in 1497.*

The few records we have of Cabot's second voyage differ slightly as to the day that the *Matthew* set sail. John Day, writing to Christopher Columbus about this voyage, says, "They left England toward the end of May [1497], and must have been on the way 35 days before sighting land. The wind was east-north-east and the sea calm going and coming back, except for one day when he [Cabot] ran into a storm two or three days before finding land."

It would seem that fortune smiled on Cabot this time around. The *Matthew* made good time across the Atlantic Ocean, with only one day of bad weather. We can only imagine how relieved and excited the crew must have been when they sighted land. But what land had they sighted? They would all have assumed it was some eastern corner of Asia. The fact that it was an entirely new continent never entered their minds. Cabot and his men were about to set foot on mainland North America.

Provisions for the voyage

You can follow John Cabot's journey on the map on pages 42–43.

Ocean-going ships of this time were small, between 59 and 98 feet (18 and 30 meters) long, and only 20 feet (6 meters) wide. The crew numbered around twenty. They needed food and water to last for several months at sea, and spare sails and ropes for emergency repairs. All this equipment took up a lot of space. They also took fresh food, including live animals. When this was finished, they moved on to meat preserved with salt and dried bread and biscuits. The men themselves had to find space on deck or below for their personal belongings and for sleeping. The captain had a cabin at the rear of the ship, where maps, charts, and **navigation** instruments were kept.

Life at sea

The crew of a ship consisted of the master (Cabot himself on the *Matthew*), master's mate (second in command), a priest, steward, cook, and carpenter, and the general crewmen who carried out the orders. Life was very hard for them, with exposure to all types of weather. A ship had to be manned 24 hours a day, so sleep was had between **watches.** The day started with prayers and a service. Poor diet often led to diseases such as scurvy. Injuries were feared because of the lack of facilities to treat them. But worst of all was the dread of a major storm. Cabot and his crew were out of sight of land for over a month, voyaging into the unknown. Their fear must have been great, in spite of the experience of the Bristol sailors in the Northern Atlantic.

The shins of a person suffering from scurvy show bleeding under the skin.

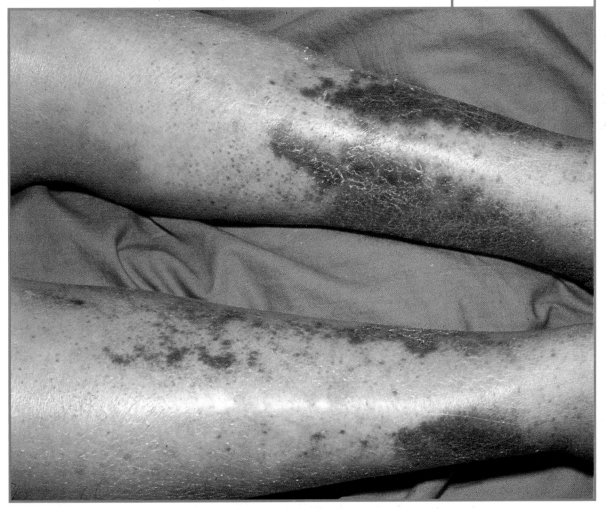

Discovering North America

You can follow John Cabot's journey on the map on pages 42–43.

Whatever land it was, it was the first Cabot and his crew had seen since losing sight of Dursey Head on the coast of Cork in Ireland. We still do not know precisely where they made their landfall. Several sites are possible. These include Nova Scotia, the Labrador coast, the Gulf of St. Lawrence, Maine, and Newfoundland. People have tried very hard to discover the truth, but so far no conclusive facts have come to light. The most likely place was Newfoundland.

The rocky coastline of Newfoundland would have been a welcome and exciting sight for Cabot and his men after about a month at sea.

In the words of a contemporary:

"This land was discovered by John Cabot the Venetian . . . in the year of the birth of our Saviour Jesus Christ 1497, on the 24th June in the morning, to which they gave the name Land First Seen . . . The people of it are dressed in the skins of animals; they use in their wars bows and arrows, lances and darts, and certain clubs of wood, and slings. It is a very sterile land. There are in it many white bears, and very large stags like horses. . . ."

An English claim

When John Cabot set foot on North American soil, he claimed it for Henry VII of England. As well as the English flag, he raised the standard of St. Mark of Venice, in memory of the city that had given him his **mariner's** skills. He did not stay long and sailed back across the Atlantic very quickly, returning to Bristol by early August 1497, just three months or so after he had set off. Although he made his finds known to the king and court, it took over 100 years for the English to make anything of the claim. Cabot brought back no treasure or other obvious signs of wealth. Had he found gold, there may well have been a flood of ships taking adventurous people out to get rich, as the Spanish did in South and Central America a few decades later, following up on the finds of Christopher Columbus. The potential of Cabot's discovery was wasted for a long time.

NAVIGATION

John Cabot would have had some very simple navigation instruments on board his ship, the *Matthew*, to help him plot his course across the wide sea. These would have included a **compass,** a **quadrant** for working out his **latitude,** a **log** for measuring the ship's speed, and a traverse table. He would have used the table to plot his course, taking measurements every half-hour. A ship's boy would have kept time with a **sandglass.**

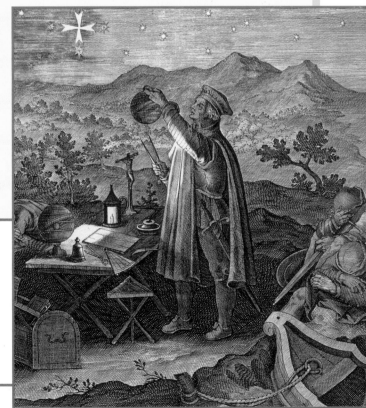

This 16th-century engraving shows the astrolabe, which was a development of the quadrant. It was used by sailors to work out their position when they were out of sight of land.

Cabot's Route of Discovery

Through documents written at the time, we can piece together something of the route Cabot is most likely to have taken. These include John Day's letter to Christopher Columbus, records and legal documents (such as the king's **patent**), and maps of the time. We can also make some educated guesses as to where Cabot landed, and perhaps the identity of the native people he encountered.

Sailing the shortest route

You can follow John Cabot's journey on the map on pages 42–43.

John Cabot, working on the idea that the earth was indeed round, sailed a far shorter distance than did Columbus. This was deliberate. He was looking for a short and efficient route to the East. Another Italian, Raimondo de Soncino, an **ambassador** at Henry VII's court, wrote to the Duke of Milan at the end of 1497. He gave some idea of the immediate direction Cabot took in his voyage: "He started from Bristol . . . passed Ireland . . . and then bore towards the north, in order to sail to the east, leaving the north on the right hand after some days . . . [John Cabot] has the description of the world in a map, and also in a solid sphere, which he had made, and shows where he has been."

This map compares Cabot's route east with Columbus's.

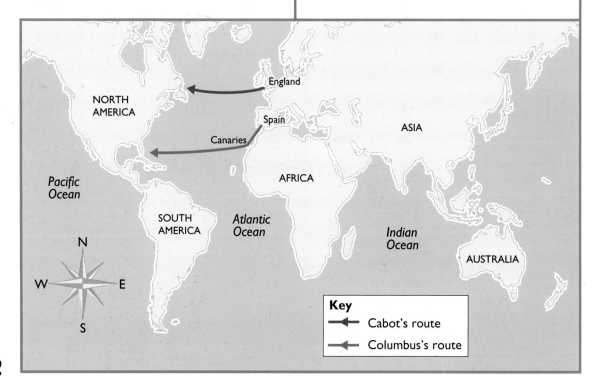

Key
— Cabot's route
— Columbus's route

The maps and "solid sphere" (globe) have unfortunately not survived. If they had, putting together the jigsaw puzzle of Cabot's voyage might have been much easier. But even if they had survived, the question of accuracy always has to be considered very carefully when dealing with descriptions that are over 500 years old. This applies to the written descriptions as well. Can we be sure that Cabot sailed for 700 leagues, as Lorenzo Pasqualigo's letter suggests? Whatever the exact details are, we can be sure of one thing—John Cabot had launched England into the great **Age of Exploration.**

Here, John and Sebastian Cabot are leaving Bristol on their first voyage of discovery in 1497. This is an early 20th-century painting, and sources differ as to whether Sebastian actually accompanied his father on this expedition.

Cabot at Court

Cabot returned to England on August 6, 1497. Four days later, he was in the presence of the king. He made the 125-mile (200-kilometer) journey from Bristol to London on the poor roads of the day almost without drawing breath at home, so eager was he to tell the king of his discoveries. His arrival caused a great stir amongst the court, and especially amongst the Spanish and Portuguese **ambassadors.** They quickly wrote back to their masters about Cabot's return from a successful voyage. They wanted to know how much of a threat the English would be in the race to gain treasure, trade, and new territories. Still no one had worked out that the discoveries of Christopher Columbus in the 1490s, and now those of Cabot, were not on Asian soil but on an entirely new landmass, the Americas.

Honor and riches

Cabot now became an English national hero and was financially rewarded. Lorenzo Pasqualigo had written that the king "has given him [Cabot] money that he may have a good time." We know from Bristol **Customs** records that Henry VII also granted Cabot an annual payment of £20 (about $30 today). This was a reasonable (though not large) sum of money that showed the king's pleasure at Cabot's discoveries. We can imagine the more comfortable home life it brought Cabot's wife and sons back in Bristol. We can also imagine the inspiration that the voyage would have been to the sons. Even a moderately successful voyage could change a man's fortunes.

This image depicts life at court in 15th-century Europe. Careers of men like Cabot could be made or destroyed by the king.

New plans

Inevitably, both the king and Cabot turned to discussing plans for future expeditions. Both saw the need to act swiftly and turn Cabot's findings to the profit of all involved. Cabot was eager to be away the next year, 1498, and this time with a proper fleet of ships. One letter reports that the king promised him ten ships, and another says fifteen or twenty. Certainly there was more confidence surrounding the planning of this next voyage. It would be a true expedition, now that the exploratory trip had been taken. Henry VII wrote a new letter of **patent** in early 1498 to give renewed royal **patronage** to the venture. In the end, five ships were appointed to the expedition, with the king and some rich London **merchants** investing in the enterprise. They set sail from Bristol in May 1498, with enough provisions to last a year.

Five fully fitted ships, like the one shown here, set out on Cabot's third and final expedition. High seas and stormy weather were always a threat to these small wooden vessels.

No Return—The Death of John Cabot

The five ships were fitted out to trade. They had on board "**merchandise** such as coarse cloth caps, laces, points (ribbon clothes fasteners) and other trifles" according to *The Great Chronicle of London*, written at the time. Cabot obviously expected to reach the East and do business with the **merchants** he found there. According to one letter, he aimed to make London an international spice trading center. Confidence could not have been higher, it would appear. He also planned to claim any land not inhabited by Christians for the king of England. This no doubt worried the Spanish and Portuguese, who thought it their right to have whatever their sailors found when voyaging west.

A bad start

Not far out of port, a storm struck the fleet. One ship was badly damaged by the storm and had to limp back to England. Cabot must have been disheartened by this bad start. However, the four remaining ships continued on their way—and they sailed not only out of sight of land but out of all historical records. For they were never seen nor heard from again. John Cabot's name dropped out of the history books.

This is Dursey Head on the coast of County Cork in Ireland, the last sight of land Cabot and his men had until they reached North America, a month later.

What happened to John Cabot?

We may never know the answer to this question. Did the ships hit a huge storm and simply sink in the North Atlantic? Or did they reach the North American coast for the second time, but for some reason not return to their native land? Some sketchy evidence exists that points to the second of these possibilities. A Portuguese expedition of 1499 traveled up the coast of North America. It returned home with seven native "Indians." A report notes that: "these men [the Indians] have . . . a piece of broken gilt sword which certainly seems to have been made in Italy. One of the boys was wearing in his ears silver rings which without a doubt seem to have been made in Venice."

Did these objects come from Cabot's expedition the year before? If so, it shows they reached America—but then what? Another theory holds that the fleet was wrecked at Grates Cove off the Newfoundland coast. Cabot and the crews swam ashore. A rock was found inscribed with the words "*Io. Cabotto*" (John Cabot) and "*Santa Maria save us*." Unfortunately this rock went missing in the 1960s, so the claim cannot be verified.

We do not know how John's wife and sons coped with their loss, nor whether they remained in Bristol or returned to their native Italy.

This is a Native American from the region that Cabot and his crew were heading for on their third and final voyage. Cabot may have landed and made contact with these people.

Sebastian Cabot

Sebastian Cabot (1476–1557) may have gone with his father on his second expedition, when he would have been about 21 years old. An account written at the time mentions his name along with that of his father. He did not go on the doomed third voyage—although his brother Sancio may well have. Sebastian lived a long and highly successful life as a **merchant,** explorer, and businessman. He had no doubt learned a great deal from his father about **navigation,** ship-building, and map-making. He became more famous in his day than his father, partly because he lived to tell the tales of his explorations.

Sebastian Cabot, the son of John Cabot, lived a long and adventurous life, ending it as governor of the Merchant Adventurers in London.

Exploring for Spain

In 1512, King Ferdinand of Spain asked Sebastian Cabot to command an expedition to North America. Cabot moved to Spain to prepare for the forthcoming voyage. However, Ferdinand died in 1516 and nothing came of these plans. For the next ten years or so, Sebastian Cabot worked for both the Spanish and the English. His most adventurous expedition took place in 1525 or 1526. He sailed to the South American coast and explored extensively the area around the La Plata **estuary** and the Paraná River. He finally returned to Spain in 1530 and spent time making maps, which included his own discoveries and those of his father.

Governor of the Merchant Adventurers

Sebastian Cabot returned to England in 1548. At about 62, he was an old man for this period. However, he still seems to have had plenty of energy left. His services were sought by many kings in Europe, eager to discover new lands and

This is an engraving of a merchant and his secretary in the 16th century, at about the time Sebastian Cabot was governor of the Merchant Adventurers.

fortunes. Sebastian Cabot's final years were taken up with a very important role as the governor of the Merchant Adventurers in London. This was a **guild** set up early in the 1400s to protect and expand the businesses of rich and powerful merchants in London. As governor, Sebastian was at the heart of English trading policies. He would have been involved with planning new expeditions, though too old to go on them. He was, for example, behind the expedition sent out in 1553 to find a northeast passage to Asia, which reached Russia.

Through Sebastian, the name of Cabot remained closely linked to the fortunes of early English **maritime** exploration and trade. By the end of the 1500s, England under Queen Elizabeth I was catching up with Spain and Portugal in terms of ambitions overseas. But the seeds were first sown by a humble but spirited citizen of Venice, who chose Bristol as his base—John Cabot.

John Cabot's Legacy

The mixed fortunes of John Cabot will not be forgotten, though he never achieved the same high standing as his contemporary explorer, Christopher Columbus. Both of these men stood at the gateway of European exploration and expansion of overseas **colonies.** John Cabot never returned from his mysterious third and final voyage across the Atlantic Ocean, so we will never know what else he may have found on behalf of his patron, Henry VII of England.

Cabot and America

An Irish monk named Brendan may have made a voyage across the Atlantic in a small boat in the 5th century. The Vikings may have made a similar voyage 500 years later and landed on

mainland North America. There are even claims that adventurous or foolish Bristol fishermen made the journey in the 15th century, following schools of cod. It is clear that John Cabot did make the voyage, at least once, and therefore has the right to claim to be the first European to stand on mainland America. This is no small claim and no insignificant legacy. He laid the foundation for what England took to be her right to colonize North America. This was followed up almost 100 years later by such great explorers as Sir Francis Drake and Sir Walter Raleigh, under the **patronage** of Queen Elizabeth I.

Sir Walter Raleigh (1552–1618) led several expeditions from England to set up colonies in North America between 1584 and 1589.

England enters the race

John Cabot put England on the map in terms of early **maritime** exploration. He introduced the more advanced **navigation** techniques developed in Italy, Spain, and Portugal, as well as maps and charts, to the backward English sailors. He became, for a very brief while, a national hero, and deservedly so. Had he returned from his fateful third voyage, his name might have been as commonly spoken as that of the better documented Christopher Columbus. But this was not to be.

*This statue of John Cabot is in Bristol, from where he embarked on the voyage that was to launch the **Age of Exploration.***

An expert mariner

John Cabot raised the standard of navigation in England. Almost every letter written about him by men of his day testifies to his skills as a sailor, **navigator,** and **cartographer.** He must have been an inspiration to the Bristol mariners and **merchants.** As Raimondo de Soncino wrote in a letter to the Duke of Milan in December 1497, Cabot arrived in England "as a foreigner and a poor man," but sailed away from her shores a man of some wealth and influence, who had the patronage of the king of a small but ambitious maritime nation, England.

Map of Cabot's route

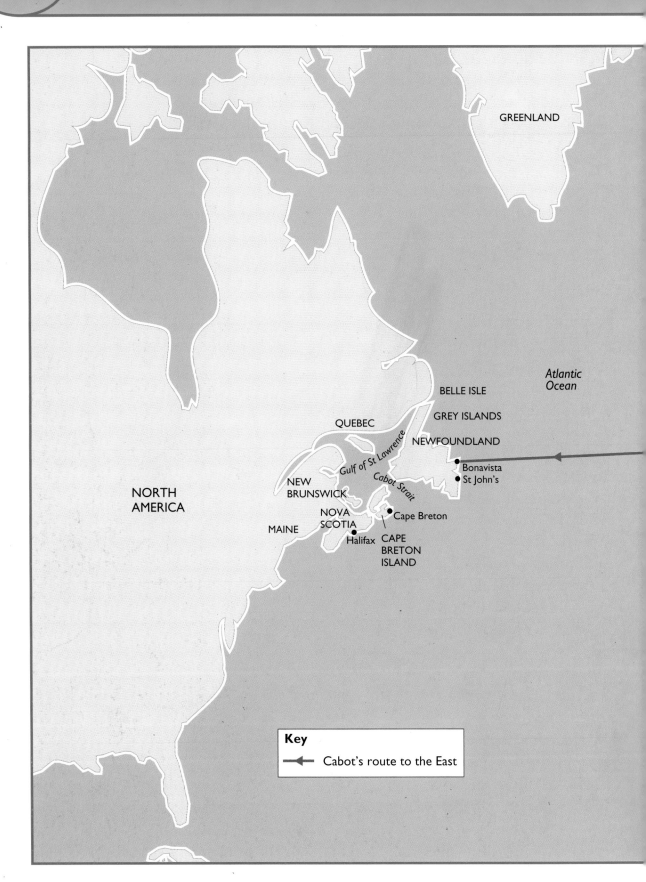

GREENLAND

Atlantic
Ocean

BELLE ISLE

GREY ISLANDS

QUEBEC

NEWFOUNDLAND

Bonavista

St John's

Gulf of St Lawrence

Cabot Strait

NEW
BRUNSWICK

NORTH
AMERICA

Cape Breton

NOVA
SCOTIA

MAINE

Halifax

CAPE
BRETON
ISLAND

Key

◄── Cabot's route to the East

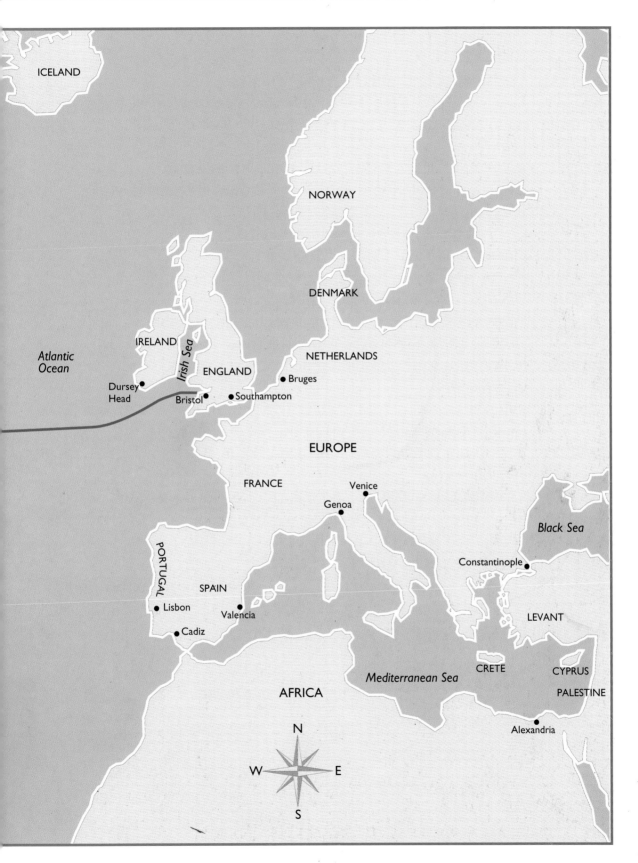

ICELAND

NORWAY

DENMARK

Atlantic Ocean

IRELAND

Irish Sea

ENGLAND

NETHERLANDS

• Bruges

• Southampton

• Bristol

Dursey Head •

EUROPE

FRANCE

Venice

Genoa

Black Sea

Constantinople •

PORTUGAL

SPAIN

• Lisbon

• Valencia

• Cadiz

LEVANT

Mediterranean Sea

CRETE

CYPRUS

PALESTINE

AFRICA

Alexandria •

N

W   E

S

Timeline

ca.1450	John Cabot (or Giovanni Caboto) is born, probably in Genoa in what is today Italy.
ca.1451	Christopher Columbus is born in Genoa.
1457	Henry VII of England is born at Pembroke Castle.
ca.1460	John Cabot's father moves his family to Venice.
ca.1474	Sebastian Cabot is born, the son of John Cabot.
1476	John Cabot, along with his father, becomes a citizen of Venice.
ca.1479	Christopher Columbus settles in Lisbon, the capital city of Portugal.
1484	Christopher Columbus moves to Spain.
1485	Henry VII becomes king of England.
ca.1490	John Cabot moves his family to Valencia in Spain.
1492	Spain takes Granada from the Moors. Christopher Columbus sets sail on his first expedition, heading west to find a new route to Asia and the East.
ca.1495	John Cabot and his family settle in Bristol, on the southwest coast of England.
1496	John Cabot sets sail on his first voyage from England to look for a passage to the East.
1497	John Cabot sets foot on North American soil, sent on the voyage by Henry VII. Vasco da Gama sails around the tip of Africa on the way to India.
1498	John Cabot and his expedition are lost, probably in the waters around the coast of North America.
1509	Henry VII dies at Richmond Palace.
1526–30	Sebastian Cabot explores the coast of Brazil for the Holy Roman Emperor, Charles V.
1557	Sebastian Cabot dies.

More Books to Read

Grolier Educational Corporation. *The Grolier Student Library of Explorers and Exploration.* Bethel, Conn.: Grolier Educational, 1998.

Larkin, Tanya. *John Cabot.* New York: Rosen Publishing Group, 2000.

Maestro, Betsy, and Giulio Maestro. *Exploration and Conquest.* New York: Morrow Avon, 1997.

Mason, Antony and Keith Lye. *The Children's Atlas of Exploration.* Brookfield, Conn.: Millbrook Press, 1993.

Polking, Kirk. *Oceanographers and Explorers of the Sea.* Berkeley Heights, N.J.: Enslow Publishers, 1999.

Ross, Stewart. *Conquerors and Explorers.* Brookfield, Conn.: Millbrook Press, 1996.

Steadwell Books, manufacturer. *John and Sebastian Cabot.* Austin, Tex.: Raintree Steck-Vaughn Publishers, 2000.

Wilbur, Keith C. *Early Explorers of North America.* Broomall, Pa.: Chelsea House Publishers, 1996.

Glossary

Age of Exploration   period from the early 15th century that lasted about 200 years, during which European explorers sailed to most parts of the globe for the first time

ambassador   person who represents his or her king, queen, or government at the court of another king or queen

ambergris   valuable wax-like substance used to make perfumes, which comes from the insides of certain whales

caravel   light and small sailing ship used in the Mediterranean Sea

cartographer   person who makes maps and globes

charter   hire a ship for money from the owner of the vessel

city state   large and important city that does not belong to a surrounding nation, but makes its own laws and governs itself

colonies   areas of land that people from another country have taken over and settled in

compass   instrument with a magnetized needle that is used to find direction

Customs   authority that collects tax for the king or government of a country from merchants who bring goods into that country

estuary   place where a river joins the sea

galley   ancient type of ship powered by both oars and sail

guild   association of merchants or craftspeople with common interests who come together for mutual support and aid

latitude   distance either north or south of the Equator (the imaginary line that goes around the widest part of the earth)

league   old-fashioned maritime measurement of distance, equal to almost 3.5 miles (about 5.5 kilometers)

log   piece of flat wood attached to a length of knotted rope used to measure the ship's speed. It was thrown over the stern into water. The faster the rope unwound, the faster the ship was traveling.

mariner   another term for a sailor

maritime   to do with the sea and sailing

merchandise   goods that are bought and sold for a profit by merchants

merchant   someone who buys and sells goods, often of one particular kind

Middle Ages   period in European history between the fall of the Roman Empire (in the 5th century) and the 15th century

monopoly   situation in which one person, company, city state, or country dominates a market for the sale of goods

Moor   name used by the Spanish for the Muslims from North Africa, who invaded their country

Muslim   member of the Islamic religion and follower of the prophet Mohammed

navigation   skill of directing the path or course of a ship

navigator   person who directs the path or course of a ship

Northwest Passage   sea route that was thought to exist in the frozen wastes of Canada that would link the Atlantic and Pacific Oceans. It was not discovered until the mid-19th century.

Orient   name given to the lands in the East, including India, China, and Japan

patent   legal document that allows a person to make money out of an invention or discovery (including new lands)

patronage   financial support given to someone by a usually wealthier, more powerful person

quadrant   instrument used by sailors to help them plot their direction in open seas

reconnaissance   usually small and lightweight advanced party that checks the route before a full-scale expedition takes place

Renaissance   period in European history between about the 15th and the 17th centuries that saw a new interest in ancient art and literature and the beginnings of modern science

republic   country that is ruled by a person who is elected, rather than by a monarch who inherits the right to rule

sandglass   time-keeping device made up of two glass bulbs, with sand trickling from one bulb to the other

shipwright   carpenter who helps build ships for a living

Spice Route and Silk Road   ancient routes, by sea and land respectively, that linked Europe with the sources of spices and silk in China, India, Japan, and the Maluku (Spice) Islands

treasury   department of government that deals with money and taxes

watch   period of time (usually four hours) when someone had to stay on duty throughout the night on board a ship

Index